My Prayer Book

Abridged Easy To Read Edition

Edited by
Victor Hoagland, C.P.

Regina Press

Nihil Obstat:	Reverend Charles Caccavale, S.T.D. Censor Librorum February 24, 2004
Imprimatur:	Most Reverend William Murphy Bishop of Rockville Centre March 1, 2004

The publishers would like to acknowledge James McGunnigle, who served and survived two tours of active combat duty in Vietnam with the First and Third Marine Divisions between 1967 and 1970.

This edition is the abridged, easy to read version of the best selling My Prayer Book. Please inquire at your local bookstore.

Scripture selections are taken from the New American Bible with Revised New Testament and Psalms Copyright © 1991, 1986, 1970 by the Confraternity of Christian Doctrine, Washington, D.C. and are used by license of the copyright owner. All rights reserved. No part of the New American Bible may be used or reproduced in any form, without permission in writing from the copyright owner.

THE REGINA PRESS
10 Hub Drive
Melville, New York 11747

All rights reserved. No part of this publication may be reproduced or transmitted in any form or by any means, electronic or mechanical, including photocopying, recording, or any information storage and retrieval system, without permission in writing from the publishers.

Artwork © Copyright 2006 by The Bridgeman Art Library.

The Bridgeman Art Library International Ltd. is registered with Companies House in England as Limited Company 33324579 of 17-19 Garway Road London W2 4PH United Kingdom. Directors: Viscountess and Viscount Bridgeman.

© Copyright 1981, 2006 by The Regina Press
Printed in Belgium.

ISBN: 0-88271-370-1

This book is dedicated to the memory of Louis F. Dempsey, a scout sniper with the First Marine Division who survived the battle for Okinawa in 1945 and the occupation of North China in 1945-1946. Believing that God had saved him for a purpose, Lou dedicated the rest of his life to his family, his country and the Roman Catholic Church.

To Lou and all the Veterans of the Armed Forces who have ever served, as well as those who are currently serving, we give our thanks. We owe all of them so much, especially those who have been and those who continue to be in harms way. On behalf of a grateful nation, we thank and honor them for their service.

Gaudenzio Ferrari. *The Last Supper, detail of Christ*, Santa Maria della Passione, Milan, Italy

Introduction

Prayer is a person-to-person *communication* with God. One who prays, converses, loves, and relates to him who has loved first. Our God has been revealed as Father, Son, and Holy Spirit, so in prayer we address and relate to three Persons, as well as to those holy people who now share fully that divine life in glory.

Prayer can take various forms. But the organ and origin of all prayer is the 'heart', that deepest part of oneself created in the image and likeness of God. Prayer can be understood as a 'heart' that overflows with joy, thanksgiving, gratitude, praise, and petition.

This is a book to help you as you pray. Prayer is for all seasons, and all occasions; prayers new and old. Some you may know already by heart; some you may welcome to see for the first time.

Many of the prayers in this book have

their origin in the great traditional devotions of the Church. Inspired by the Holy Spirit, nourished by the holy lives and desires of countless faithful Christians, they come to help us in our turn to be a people close to our God. Like bread for the hungry, like water for the thirsting, prayer brings strength and peace to the hours of our day and the years of our life. Prayer at the same time is a personal response to God's presence. Thus, before saying any of the following prayers, let the one who prays acknowledge God's presence and then open his or her heart in words of faith, hope, and love.

The Holy Eucharist

At the Last Supper Jesus gave us his Body and Blood. On the night he was betrayed, he took bread in his hands, gave thanks to God, and gave it to his disciples saying: "Take and eat, this is my body." Then he took a cup of wine, again giving thanks, and gave it to his friends, saying: "Take and drink. This is the cup of my blood, which will be shed for you and for all, so that sins may be forgiven. Do this in memory of me."

Whenever we celebrate the Holy Eucharist, Jesus Christ, who is all our good, is with us as we remember him. With him, we give God thanks for the blessings of creation, of redemption and salvation. Through him, we receive God's love and grace, as he draws us together and fills our minds with the promises of life eternal.

In the Holy Eucharist, we remember the mystery of the death and resurrection of Jesus, which recalls the sacrifice he made for us and the powerful love of God that is stronger than death itself. After his resurrection, Jesus' first disciples recognized him "in the breaking of the bread." Today we recognize him in this action too. Our celebration of the Eucharist is a privileged time for listening to him in the scriptures, for receiving him in the sacrament, and for gathering with others who believe in him.

The Holy Eucharist is the center and source of the Church's life. It is described by many terms. It is called Eucharist, because it is an action of thanksgiving; the Breaking of the Bread, because Jesus offers his blessings through these signs; the Holy Sacrifice, because it recalls the sacrifice of Jesus for us; Holy Communion, because it unites us to Christ; Holy Mass, because it sends us forth to do God's will in our daily lives.

Like the manna once given to the Israelites in the desert, the Eucharist is food for our journey. Like the bread Jesus once gave to the multitude in Galilee, it is a sign of God's love that is beyond anything we can expect.

Prayers Before Communion

Jesus, the Bread of Life

Father in heaven,
> you have made us for yourself;
> our hearts are restless
> until they rest in you.

Fulfill this longing through Jesus
> the bread of life,
> so that we may witness to him
> who alone satisfies the hungers
> of the human family.

By the power of your Spirit
> lead us to the heavenly table
> where we may feast on the vision
> of your glory for ever and ever.
> Amen.

Michelangelo Merisi da Caravaggio. *The Supper at Emmaus, 1606*, Pinacoteca di Brera, Milan, Italy

Prayer Before Holy Communion

Come, O blessed Savior, and nourish
my soul with heavenly Food,
the Food which contains every
sweetness and every delight.
Come, Bread of angels, and satisfy
the hunger of my soul.
Come, glowing Furnace of charity,
and enkindle in my heart
the flame of divine love.
Come, Light of the world,
and enlighten the darkness
of my mind.
Come, King of kings, and make me
obedient to your holy will.
Come, loving Savior,
and make me meek and humble.
Come, Friend of the sick, and heal
the infirmities of my body and
the weakness of my soul.
Come good Shepherd,
my God and my all,
and take me to yourself.

Prayer to the Virgin Mary

Mother of mercy and love,
blessed Virgin Mary, I am a poor and unworthy sinner, and I turn to you in confidence and love.
You stood by your Son
as he hung dying on the cross.
Stand also by me, a poor sinner,
and by all the priests who are offering Mass today here and throughout the entire Church.
Help us to offer a perfect and acceptable sacrifice
in the sight of the holy and undivided Trinity,
our most high God. Amen.

Prayer of St. Thomas Aquinas

Almighty and ever-living God,
I approach the sacrament of your only begotten Son,
our Lord Jesus Christ.
I come sick to the Doctor of life,

unclean to the Fountain of mercy,
blind to the radiance of eternal Light,
and poor and needy to the Lord of
heaven and earth.
Lord, in your great generosity,
heal my sickness,
   wash away my defilement,
enlighten my blindness,
   enrich my poverty,
and clothe my nakedness.
May I receive the Bread of angels,
the King of kings and Lord of lords,
with humble reverence,
with the purity and faith,
the repentance and love, and the
   determined purpose
that will help to bring me to salvation.
May I receive the Sacrament of the
Lord's body and blood,
and its reality and power.
Kind God,
may I receive the Body of your only
   begotten Son, our Lord Jesus Christ,
born from the womb
of the Virgin Mary,

and so be received into his mystical
body and numbered among
his members.
Loving Father,
as on my earthly pilgrimage
I now receive your beloved Son
under the veil of a Sacrament, may I
one day see him face to face in glory,
who lives and reigns with you forever.
   Amen.

Prayer of St. Ambrose

Lord Jesus Christ,
I approach your banquet table in fear
and trembling, for I am a sinner,
and dare not rely on my own worth
but only on your goodness and mercy.
I am defiled by many sins
   in body and soul,
and by my unguarded thoughts
   and words.
Gracious God of majesty and awe,
I seek your protection,
I look for your healing.

Poor troubled sinner that I am,
I appeal to you,
the Fountain of all mercy.
I cannot bear your judgment,
but I trust in your salvation.
Lord, I show my wounds to you
and uncover my shame before you.
I know my sins are many and great,
and they fill me with fear,
but I hope in your mercies,
for they cannot be numbered.
Lord Jesus Christ, eternal King,
 God and man,
crucified for mankind,
look upon me with mercy and hear
 my prayer,
for I trust in you.
Have mercy on me,
full of sorrow and sin,
for the depth of your compassion
 never ends.
Praise to you, saving sacrifice,
offered on the wood of the cross for me
 and for all mankind.
Praise to the noble and precious blood,

flowing from the wounds of my crucified Lord Jesus Christ
and washing away the sins of the whole world.
Remember, Lord, your creature, whom you have redeemed with your blood.
I repent my sins, and I long to put right what I have done.
Merciful Father, take away all my offenses and sins;
purify me in body and soul,
and make me worthy to taste the holy of holies.
May your body and blood, which I intend to receive, although I am unworthy, be for me the remission of my sins, the washing away of my guilt, the end of my evil thoughts, and the rebirth of my better instincts. May it incite me to do the works pleasing to you and profitable to my health in body and soul, and be a firm defense against the wiles of my enemies. Amen.

Prayers After Communion

Prayer to the Virgin Mary

Mary, holy Virgin Mother,
I have received your Son,
>Jesus Christ.
With love you became his Mother,
gave birth to him, nursed him,
and helped him grow to manhood.
With love I return him to you,
to hold once more, to love with all
>your heart, and to offer to the
>Holy Trinity as our supreme act
>of worship for your honor and
>for the good of all your pilgrim
>brothers and sisters.

Mother, ask God to forgive my sins
and to help me serve him more
>faithfully.
Keep me true to Christ until death,
and let me come to praise him with
>you for ever and ever.
Amen.

Prayer to Our Redeemer

Jesus, may all that is you
 flow into me.
May your body and blood be my
 food and drink.
May your passion and death be my
 strength and life.
Jesus, with you by my side enough
 has been given.
May the shelter I seek be the shadow
 of your cross.
Let me not run from the love which
 you offer, but hold me safe
 from the forces of evil.
On each of my dyings shed your
 light and your love.
Keep calling to me until that day
 comes, when, with your saints,
 I may praise you for ever. Amen.

The Anima Christi

Soul of Christ, sanctify me.
Body of Christ, save me.
Blood of Christ, inebriate me.
Water from the side of Christ, wash me.
Passion of Christ, strengthen me.
O good Jesus, hear me.
Within your wounds, hide me.
Permit me never to be separated
   from you.
From the malignant enemy, defend me.
In the hour of my death, call me
   and bid me to come to you,
      that with your saints, I may praise
      you for ever and ever. Amen.

Prayer to Jesus Christ Crucified

My good and dear Jesus,
I kneel before you
asking you most earnestly
to engrave upon my heart
a deep and lively faith,
   hope, and charity,

with true repentance for my sins,
and a firm resolve to make amends.
As I reflect upon your five wounds,
and dwell upon them with deep compassion and grief,
I recall, good Jesus, the words the
> prophet David spoke
long ago concerning yourself:
they have pierced my hands and feet,
they have counted all my bones!

Prayer of St. Thomas Aquinas

Lord,
Father all-powerful and ever-living God,
I thank you, for even though I am a sinner, your unprofitable servant, not because of my worth but in the kindness of your mercy, you have fed me with the precious body and blood of your Son,
> our Lord Jesus Christ.
I pray that this Holy Communion may not bring me condemnation and punishment but forgiveness

and salvation.
May it be a helmet of faith
and a shield of good will.
May it purify me from evil ways
and put an end to my evil passions.
May it bring me charity and patience,
humility and obedience,
and growth in the power to do good.
May it be my strong defense
against all my enemies, visible
and invisible, and the perfect
calming of all my evil impulses,
bodily and spiritual.
May it unite me more closely to you,
the one true God, and lead me safely
through death to everlasting happiness
with you. And I pray that you will
lead me, a sinner, to the banquet where
you, with your Son and Holy Spirit,
are true and perfect light,
total fulfillment, everlasting joy,
gladness without end,
and perfect happiness to your saints.
Grant this through Christ our Lord.
Amen.

Act of Thanksgiving

From the depths of my heart
 I thank you, Lord, for your
 infinite kindness in coming to me.
 How good you are to me!
 With your most holy Mother and
 the angels, I praise your mercy
 and generosity toward me.
I thank you for nourishing my soul
 with your sacred body and
 precious blood.
I will try to show my gratitude to
 you in the Sacrament of your
 love, by loving obedience
 to your holy commandments,
 by fidelity to my duties,
 by kindness to my neighbor and
 by an earnest endeavor to
 become more like you in my
 daily conduct.
Grant that I may spend the hours
 of the day gladly working with
 you according to your will.
May I not lose my enthusiasm

in serving you.
May my conversations
 be occasions of charity.
May I be patient with myself and
 those around me in the day's
 disappointments.
May I be mindful of others
 rather than myself in moments
 of fatigue and illness.
May I be generous and faithful so
 that when this day is over I may
 feel that life is really meaningful
 and peaceful for it has been spent
 in your loving company. Amen.

Prayer of Self-Dedication to Jesus Christ

Lord Jesus Christ, take all my freedom, my memory, my understanding,
 and my will. All that I have and
 cherish you have given me.
I surrender it all to be guided by
 your will.

Your grace and your love are wealth enough for me.
Give me these, Lord Jesus, and I ask for nothing more.

Prayer for Love of God

O great Lord of heaven and earth, infinite good and majesty, you who have loved men so tenderly, how is it that you are despised by so many human beings? You have loved me in a special manner and have bestowed many wonderful graces on me.
Yet I, too, have despised you by every sin through which I have turned against your law. I resolve this day to love you with my whole heart and to love nothing unless it can be loved in you. Grant me this gift of love: a fervent love that will make me reject the appeal of sinful creatures; a strong love that will make me conquer all difficulties to please you; a persevering love that will never be dissolved. Amen.

Brief Statement of Christian Doctrine

The Core of Christian Faith

Yes, Jesus Christ is our Teacher and Lord. His life and words draw men and women of every age and nation to his side. No other great figure of history approaches what he said and did.

Born poor, his childhood spent in an obscure Galilaean village, he suddenly emerged for a few dazzling years to teach and work wonders in the Jewish world of his time. He was opposed by those in power who brought him to trial and crucified him. After three days he rose from the dead.

Those who were witnesses to his resurrection told the good news to others. They were convinced he was the Son of God who came to bring new life and hope to a world lost in darkness. He would bring a new kingdom, a new order, based on justice and love. Jesus promised to remain always with his Church. Receiving the Holy Spirit, his Church would proclaim his life and words.

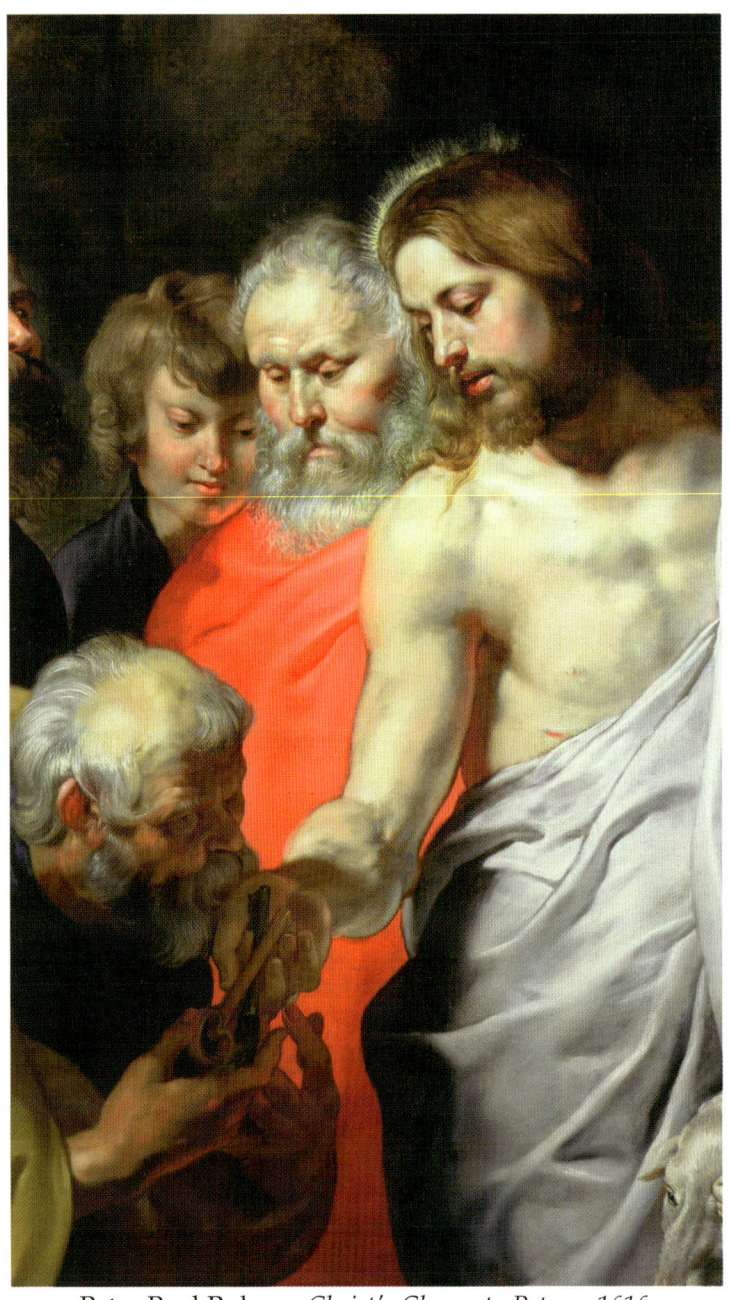

Peter Paul Rubens. *Christ's Charge to Peter, c.1616*, Wallace Collection, London, UK

The Sacraments

The Catholic Church seeks to remain one with Jesus Christ in a variety of ways. One of these is the sacraments — seven great signs that mark the different stages and events in human life. From birth till death, the follower of Jesus reaches out to him for power and life to love and live as he did. The sacraments are key events for Christ to draw men and women more fully into his saving actions. These ritual acts of human communication and human worship in the Church are events of grace in which the Spirit of God is imparted by the Lord who is ever sending his Spirit into the world. Through the sacraments Jesus is always present to those who believe in him.

They are: **Baptism**
  Confirmation
  Eucharist
  Reconciliation
  Anointing of the Sick
  Matrimony
  Holy Orders

The Beatitudes

Jesus promised happiness to those who believe in him and follow his teaching. He summed up his promises in his Sermon on the Mount. What he taught there, he lived himself, and the stories and events of the New Testament re-echo these same central truths. The Beatitudes are a summary of the different directions in life that lead to the peace and happiness promised by Jesus. The traditional listing of the beatitudes is:

1. Blessed are the poor in spirit: the reign of God is theirs.
2. Blessed are the sorrowing: they shall be consoled.
3. Blessed are the lowly: they shall inherit the land.
4. Blessed are they who hunger and thirst for holiness: they shall have their fill.
5. Blessed are they who show mercy: mercy shall be theirs.
6. Blessed are the single-hearted: for

they shall see God.
7. Blessed are the peacemakers: they shall be called sons of God.
8. Blessed are those persecuted for holiness' sake: the reign of God is theirs.

The Works of Mercy

Jesus told us to love one another as he loved us. His own life revealed his loving concern and compassion for the poor, the sick, and the troubled. The leper isolated from society, the blind man alone in his darkness, the frightened woman taken in adultery, the thief condemned to a cross found in him care, support, and strength. He advised those who would follow him to make their love as practical and selfless as his own. The corporal and spiritual works of mercy are guidelines for Christian love.

The Corporal Works of Mercy

To feed the hungry.
To give drink to the thirsty.
To clothe the naked.
To visit and ransom the captives.
To shelter the homeless.
To visit the sick.
To bury the dead.

The Spiritual Works of Mercy

To admonish sinners.
To instruct the ignorant.
To counsel the doubtful.
To comfort the sorrowful.
To bear wrongs patiently.
To forgive all injuries.
To pray for the living and the dead.

The Ten Commandments

Jesus reaffirmed the law that Moses, inspired by God, gave to the Jewish people. He came, he said, not to destroy the law but to fulfill it. Through the centuries the Judeo-Christian moral code has become a basic guideline for human conduct.

The human family left to its own wisdom often pursues a course of violence and destruction. The human heart, whose ways are "torturous" according to the Prophet Jeremiah, is prone to contraction and selfishness. "For from the heart come evil thoughts, murder, adultery, unchastity, theft, false witness, blasphemy" (Mt. 15:19).

The Ten Commandments warn of human deception and at the same time point out the proper way for one to live. Following Jesus Christ means to follow their teaching.

1. I, the Lord, am your God. You shall not have other gods besides me.
2. You shall not take the name of the Lord, your God, in vain.

3. Remember to keep holy the Sabbath Day.
4. Honor your father and your mother.
5. You shall not kill.
6. You shall not commit adultery.
7. You shall not steal.
8. You shall not bear false witness against your neighbor.
9. You shall not covet your neighbor's wife.
10. You shall not covet anything that belongs to your neighbor.

The Greatest Commandment of All

"When the Pharisees heard that he had silenced the Sadducees, they gathered together, and one of them [a scholar of the law] tested him by asking, 'Teacher, which commandment in the law is the greatest?' He said to him, 'You shall love the Lord, your God, with all your heart, with all your soul, and with all your mind. This is the greatest and the first commandment. The second is like it: You shall love your neighbor as yourself. The whole law and the prophets depend on these two commandments.' "

Mt. 22:34-40

Ecclesiastical Laws

It is in Christ that authority of the Church dwells. The laws of the Church and the legitimate commands of the pope and bishops are issued with the authority Christ gave to the Church for the good of the people of God. The bishops of each country generally list the most notable of special duties of Catholics as "precepts of the Church." The bishops of the United States have endorsed the following for their people. (Those traditionally mentioned as precepts of the Church are marked with an asterisk.)

1. To keep holy the day of the Lord's resurrection: to worship God by participating in Mass every Sunday

and Holy Day of Obligation: * to avoid those activities that would hinder renewal of soul and body, e.g., need less work and business activities, unnecessary shopping, etc.

2. To lead a sacramental life: to receive Holy Communion frequently and the Sacrament of Reconciliation regularly – minimally, to receive the Sacrament of Reconciliation at least once a year (annual confession is obligatory only if serious sin is involved). *– minimally, to receive Holy Communion at least once a year, between the first Sunday of Lent and Trinity Sunday.

3. To study Catholic teaching in preparation for the Sacrament of Confirmation, to be confirmed, and then to continue to study and advance the cause of Christ.

4. To observe the marriage laws of the Church: * to give religious training (by example and word) to one's children; to use parish schools and

religious education programs.
5. To strengthen and support the Church: *one's own parish community and parish priests; the worldwide Church and the Holy Father.
6. To do penance, including abstaining from meat and fasting from food on the appointed days. *
7. To join in the missionary spirit and apostolate of the Church.

Holy Days of Obligation in the United States

1. All Sundays of the year.
2. January 1 – Solemnity of Mary, the Mother of God.*
3. Ascension Thursday – Forty days after Easter. In some regions of the United States, the Holy See has granted an indult to move the Solemnity of the Ascension to the seventh Sunday of Easter.
4. August 15 – Assumption of the Blessed Virgin Mary.*

5. November 1 – All Saints' Day.*
6. December 8 – The Immaculate Conception.
7. December 25 – Christmas Day.

* If the Holy Days of January 1, August 15 and November 1 fall on a Saturday or a Monday, there is no obligation to attend Mass, but all Catholics are encouraged to do so.

Fast and Abstinence

The obligation to fast allows Catholics from ages twenty-one to fifty-nine to have one full meal and two smaller meals during a day of fast. The obligation to abstain does not allow Catholics from the age of fourteen and older to eat meat on days of abstinence.

Ash Wednesday and Good Friday are days of fast and abstinence, while all Fridays during Lent are days of abstinence. The regulations concerning fast and abstinence vary from diocese to diocese.

Everyday Prayers

Sign of the Cross

In the name of the Father,
and of the Son, ✝
and of the Holy Spirit.
 Amen.

The Lord's Prayer

Our Father, who art in heaven,
hallowed be thy name;
thy kingdom come;
thy will be done on earth
 as it is in heaven.
Give us this day our daily bread;
and forgive us our trespasses
as we forgive those who trespass
against us; and lead us not into
temptation, but deliver us from evil.
Amen.

Philippe de Champaigne. *The Good Shepherd*, (c.1650-60)
Musee des Beaux-Arts, Tours, France

The Hail Mary

Hail Mary, full of grace,
>the Lord is with thee.
>Blessed art thou among women,
>and blessed is the fruit
>of thy womb, Jesus.
Holy Mary, Mother of God,
>pray for us sinners,
>now and at the hour of our death.
Amen.

Glory Be to the Father

Glory be to the Father, and to the Son,
>and to the Holy Spirit.
As it was in the beginning, is now and ever shall be, world without end. Amen.

Grace Before Meals

Bless us, O Lord, and these your gifts which we are about to receive from your bounty, through Christ our Lord. Amen.

Grace After Meals

We give you thanks, almighty God,
for these and all your blessings;
you live and reign for ever
and ever. Amen.

Come Holy Spirit

Come, Holy Spirit,
fill the hearts of your faithful and
kindle in them the fire of your love.
Send forth your Spirit, and they shall
be created; and you will renew
the face of the earth.
O God, on the first Pentecost you
instructed the hearts of those
who believed in you by the light
of the Holy Spirit; under the
inspiration of the same Spirit,
give us a taste for what is right
and true and a continuing sense
of his presence and power;
through Jesus Christ our Lord.
Amen.

An Act of Faith

O God,
I firmly believe all the truths that you have revealed and that you teach us through your Church, for you are truth itself and can neither deceive nor be deceived.

An Act of Hope

O God,
I hope with complete trust that you will give me, through the merits of Jesus Christ, all the necessary grace in this world and everlasting life in the world to come, for this is what you have promised and you always keep your promises.

An Act of Charity

O God,
I love you with my whole heart above all things, because you are infinitely good; and for your sake I love my neighbor as I love myself.

The Apostles' Creed

I believe in God, the Father almighty,
Creator of heaven and earth.
I believe in Jesus Christ, his only Son,
our Lord.
He was conceived by the power of
the Holy Spirit and born
of the Virgin Mary.
He suffered under Pontius Pilate,
was crucified, died and was buried.
He descended to the dead.
On the third day he rose again.
He ascended into heaven,
and is seated at the right hand
of the Father.
He will come again to judge
the living and the dead.
I believe in the Holy Spirit,
the holy catholic Church,
the communion of saints,
the forgiveness of sins,
the resurrection of the body,
and life everlasting.
Amen.

Guiseppe Cesari. *The Transfiguration*,
Ferens Art Gallery, Hull City Museums and Art Galleries, UK

The Confiteor

I confess to almighty God, and to you,
my brothers and sisters, that I have
sinned through my own fault, in my
thoughts and in my words, in what I
have done, and in what I have failed
to do; and I ask blessed Mary, ever
Virgin, all the angels and saints,
and you, my brothers and sisters,
to pray for me to the Lord our God.

Act of Contrition

My God, I am sorry for my sins
with all my heart.
In choosing to do wrong and failing
to do good, I have sinned against you
whom I should love above all things.
I firmly intend with your help, to do
penance, to sin no more, and to
avoid whatever leads me to sin.
Our Savior Jesus Christ
suffered and died for us.
In his name, my God, have mercy.

Devotions to the Sacred Heart of Jesus

Devotions to the Sacred Heart of Jesus

St. Margaret Mary Alacoque was born in France in 1647 and died in 1690. Our Lord appeared to St. Margaret Mary several times during her life as a nun in the Visitation Order. In 1675, the great revelation was made to St. Margaret Mary that she, along with Father de la Colombiere, S.J., was to be the chief instrument for instituting the Feast of the Sacred Heart and for spreading devotion to the Sacred Heart throughout the world.

The Great Promise of the First Friday

All who receive Holy Communion on nine consecutive First Fridays have been blessed by our Lord with the grace of a most wonderful promise. We should listen carefully. It is our Savior, himself, who speaks to us through St. Margaret Mary:

"I promise you in the unfathomable mercy of my heart that my omnipotent love will procure the grace of final penitence for all those who communicate on nine successive First Fridays of the month; they will not die in my disfavor, or without having received their sacraments, since my divine heart will be their sure refuge in the last moments of their life."

Our Lord also told St. Margaret Mary of the following additional blessings:

1. I will give them all the graces necessary for their state of life.
2. I will establish peace in their families.
3. I will comfort them in all their afflictions.
4. I will be their secure refuge during life, and above all in death.
5. I will bestow a special blessing upon all their undertakings.
6. Sinners shall find in my heart the source and infinite ocean of mercy.
7. Tepid souls shall grow fervent.
8. Fervent souls shall quickly mount to high perfection.
9. I will bless every place where a picture of my heart shall be exposed and honored.
10. I will give to priests the gift of

touching the most hardened hearts.
11. Those who shall promote this devotion shall have their names written in my heart – never to be blotted out.

Act of Reparation to the Sacred Heart of Jesus

O sweet Jesus, whose overflowing charity for men is requited by so much forgetfulness, negligence, and contempt, behold us prostrate before you eager to repair by a special act of homage the cruel indifference and injuries to which your loving heart is everywhere subject.

Mindful alas! That we ourselves have had a share in such great indignities, which we now deplore from the depth of our heart, we humbly ask your pardon and declare our readiness to atone by voluntary expiation not only for our own personal offenses but also for the sins of those, who, straying far from the path of salvation, refuse in their obstinate infidelity to follow you, their shepherd and leader, or, renouncing the vows of their baptism, have cast off the sweet yoke of your law.

We are now resolved to expiate each and every deplorable outrage committed against you. We are determined to make amends for the manifold offenses against Christian modesty in unbecoming dress and behavior, for all the foul seductions laid to ensnare the feet of the innocent, for the frequent violation of Sundays and holy days, and the shocking blasphemies uttered against you and your saints.

We wish also to make amends for the insults to which your vicar on earth and your priests are subjected, for the profanation, by conscious neglect or terrible acts of sacrilege, of the very sacrament of your divine love; and lastly for the public crimes of nations who resist the rights and the teaching authority of the Church which you have founded.

Would, O divine Jesus, we were able to wash away such abominations with our blood! We now offer in reparation for these violations of your divine honor, the satisfaction you did once make to your eternal Father on the Cross and which you continue to renew daily before us; we offer it in union with the acts of atonement of your virgin mother and all the saints and of the pious faithful on earth; and we sincerely promise to make recompense as far as we can with the help of your grace, for all neglect of your great love and for the sins we and others have committed in the past.

Henceforth we will live a life of unwavering faith, of purity of conduct, of perfect observance of the precepts of the Gospel and especially that of charity.

We promise to the best of our power to prevent others from offending you and to bring as many as possible to follow you.

O loving Jesus, through the intercession of the Blessed Virgin Mary, our model in reparation, deign to receive the voluntary offering we make of this act of expiation; and by the crowning gift of perseverance keep us faithful unto death in our duty and the allegiance we owe to you, so that we may all one day come to that happy home, where you with the Father and the Holy Spirit live and reign, God, world without end. Amen.

Act of Consecration of the Human Race to the Sacred Heart

Most sweet Jesus, Redeemer of the human race, look down upon us humbly prostrate before you. We are yours, and yours we wish to be; but to be more surely united with you, behold each one of us freely consecrates himself today to your most Sacred Heart. Many indeed have never known you; many too, despising your precepts, have rejected you. Have mercy on them all, most merciful Jesus, and draw them to your Sacred Heart. Be King, O Lord, not only of the faithful who have never forsaken you, but also of the prodigal children who have abandoned you; grant that they may quickly return to their Father's house lest they die of wretchedness and hunger. Be King of those who are deceived by erroneous opinions, or whom discord holds aloof, and call them back to the harbor of truth and unity of faith, so that soon there may be but one flock and one shepherd. Grant, O Lord, to your Church assurance of freedom and immunity from harm; give peace and order to all nations, and make the earth resound from pole to pole with one cry: "Praise to the Divine Heart that wrought our salvation; to it be glory and honor for ever." Amen.

Litany of the Sacred Heart of Jesus

Lord, have mercy, Christ, have mercy, Lord, have mercy. Christ, hear us.
Christ, graciously hear us.
God the Father of heaven,
– Have mercy on us.
God the Son, Redeemer of the world.
(After each invocation, respond with, "Have mercy on us.")
God the Holy Spirit,
Holy Trinity, one God,
Heart of Jesus, Son of the eternal Father,
Heart of Jesus, formed by the Holy Spirit in the womb of the Virgin Mary,
Heart of Jesus,
united with God's eternal Word,
Heart of Jesus, of limitless majesty,

Heart of Jesus, temple of God among us,
Heart of Jesus, shrine of the Most High,
Heart of Jesus,
   house of God and gate of heaven,
Heart of Jesus, glowing with love for us,
Heart of Jesus, overflowing with
   goodness and love,
Heart of Jesus, full of kindness and love,
Heart of Jesus, Fountain of all holiness,
Heart of Jesus, worthy of all praise,
Heart of Jesus,
King and Center of all hearts,
Heart of Jesus, Treasure-house of
   wisdom and knowledge,
Heart of Jesus,
Tabernacle of God's fullness,
Heart of Jesus,
   in whom the Father is well pleased,
Heart of Jesus, of whose fullness
   we have all received,
Heart of Jesus,
   desire of the everlasting hills,
Heart of Jesus, patient and full of mercy,
Heart of Jesus,
   generous to all who turn to you,

Heart of Jesus, Source of life and
holiness,
Heart of Jesus, Atonement for our sins,
Heart of Jesus,
overwhelmed with reproaches,
Heart of Jesus, bruised for our sins,
Heart of Jesus,
obedient all the way to death,
Heart of Jesus, pierced with a lance,
Heart of Jesus,
Source of all consolation,
Heart of Jesus, our Life and
Resurrection,
Heart of Jesus,
our Peace and Reconciliation,
Heart of Jesus, Sacrifice for sin,
Heart of Jesus,
Salvation of all who trust in you,
Heart of Jesus,
Hope of all who die in you,
Heart of Jesus, Delight of all the saints,
Lamb of God, you take away
the sins of the world,
– Spare us, O Lord,
Lamb of God you take away the sins of

the world,
– Graciously hear us, O Lord.
Lamb of God, you take away the sins of the world,
– Have mercy on us.
Jesus, gentle and humble of heart,
– Touch our hearts and make them like your own.

Let us pray.

Father, we rejoice in the gifts of love we have received from the heart of Jesus your Son. Open our hearts to share his life and continue to bless us with his love.
We ask this through Lord Jesus Christ, your Son, who lives and reigns with you and the Holy Spirit, one God, for ever and ever.

Novena Prayers

The evangelist Luke recounts that after the ascension of the risen Lord, the apostles together with Mary, the disciples, and the women from Galilee spent nine days in prayer. They looked forward to a new presence of Jesus through the Spirit. These nine days of prayer and expectation led to the custom of praying for special intentions during a period of nine days. Such a period of prayer is called a novena. Novenas have become sources of inspiration and piety for people of faith who find themselves in need.

In Honor of
Our Lady of the Miraculous Medal

The devotion was begun by Catherine Laboure, a French religious sister. She experienced a number of apparitions of Mary. In one, Catherine saw a picture of Mary standing on a globe with light streaming from her hands. Around the Virgin were the words: "O Mary conceived without sin, pray for us who have recourse to you." Mary entrusted to Catherine the inauguration of this devotion.

Johann Ulrich Loth. *St. Luke,* (c.1590-1662)
Wilanow Palace, Warsaw, Poland

O Immaculate Virgin Mary, Mother of our Lord Jesus and our Mother, penetrated with the most lively confidence in your all-powerful and never-failing intercession, manifested so often through the Miraculous Medal, we your loving and trustful children implore you to obtain for us the graces and favors we ask during this Novena, if they be beneficial to our immortal souls, and the souls for whom we pray. *(Here privately mention your petitions.)*

You know, O Mary, how often our souls have been the sanctuaries of your Son who hates iniquity.

Obtain for us then a deep hatred of sin and that purity of heart which will attach us to God alone so that our every thought, word, and deed may tend to his greater glory.

Obtain for us a spirit of prayer and self-denial that we may recover by penance what we have lost by sin and at length attain to that blessed abode where you are the Queen of angels and of men. Amen.

An Act of Consecration to Our Lady of the Miraculous Medal

O Virgin Mother of God, Mary Immaculate, we dedicate and consecrate ourselves to you under the title of Our Lady of the Miraculous Medal.

May this Medal be for each one of us a sure sign of your affection for us and a constant reminder of our duties toward you.

Ever while wearing it, may we be blessed by your loving protection and preserved in the grace of your Son.

O most powerful Virgin, Mother of our Savior, keep us close to you every moment of our lives.

Obtain for us, your children, the grace of a happy death; so that, in union with you, we may enjoy the bliss of heaven for ever. Amen.

O Mary, conceived without sin, pray for us who have recourse to you. *(3 times.)*

In Honor of The Immaculate Conception

Mary is part of the mystery of Christ. Inspired by the Spirit of God, the Church grows in its understanding of this mystery and its richness.Thus the Church gradually arrives at the truth of different aspects of Mary's holiness. One such aspect is her Immaculate Conception. Mary was full of grace and free from original sin at the very beginning of her existence as a human person in her mother's womb. This was in anticipation of the merits of her Son. She was thus able to give herself wholeheartedly to her Son's work.

O Mary Immaculate, lily of purity, I salute you, because from the very first instant of your conception you were filled with grace. I thank and adore the most Holy Trinity for having imparted such sublime favors upon you.

O Mary, full of grace, help me to share, even though just a little, in the fullness of grace so wonderfully bestowed upon you in your Immaculate Conception.

Bartolome Esteban Murillo. *The Immaculate Conception*,
Museo de Bellas Artes, Seville, Spain

With firm confidence in your never failing intercession, we beseech you to obtain for us the intention of this novena *(here mention your request)*, and also that purity of mind, heart, and body necessary to unite us with God. Amen.

O Mary, conceived without sin, pray for us who have recourse to you.

O Mother of God, by your Immaculate Conception, intercede for us with your divine Son, and obtain for us from him, the favor for which we pray.

In Honor of St. Anne

Nothing is known for certain about Anne, the mother of Mary. There is a legend about her that closely parallels the story of the mother of Samuel in the Old Testament. Anne, like the mother of Samuel, was childless and earnestly prayed for a child. Her prayer was answered and she saw her child as a gift from God. She thus invites believers to place their lives in the hands of God alone.

St. Anne, you are the mother of Mary, the Queen of heaven and earth.
During your lifetime you gave her a powerful example of love and concern.
I venerate your memory and beg your assistance.
Be concerned for me and act as my intercessor.
I ask for health of body and soul, a joyful acceptance of God's will for me and in particular *(here mention your request).*
Give me and those for whom I pray the strength to carry our cross in the spirit of Jesus and so live and die in his love. Amen.

Master of 1518. *Madonna and Child with St. Anne*,
Private Collection

Francisco de Zurbaran. *St. Anthony of Padua*, (1598-1664)
Prado, Madrid, Spain

In Honor of St. Anthony of Padua

Anthony devoted his ministry to preaching in Italy and France at a time when the Church was refuting many heresies. Although he is known as the finder of lost articles, he was really one of the greatest preachers in the history of the Church.

St. Anthony, during your lifetime you were always gracious to poor sinners who sought the comfort of your ministry.

You had the happiness of holding in your arms our blessed Lord under the guise of a little child and at times the power of God enabled you to be an instrument of miraculous events.

Be gracious to me and intercede with our Lord for the petition I now make with such ardent desire *(here mention your request).*

As a pledge of my gratitude accept my promise to live more in harmony with the values of the Gospel and to be more devoted to the service of the poor whom you loved so deeply.

Bless this resolution and help me to be faithful. Amen.

In Honor of St. Jude

Jude was the apostle who asked the Lord at the Last Supper why he had manifested himself only to his disciples and not to the whole world. Postscriptural tradition asserts that Jude preached the Gospel and suffered martyrdom in Mesopotamia. In time Jude came to be regarded as the special patron of "hopeless cases", possibly due to the fact that devotion to him had been neglected since he had the same name as the apostle who betrayed Jesus.

St. Jude, your life was enriched with the friendship of our Lord Jesus and with his call to be one of the twelve apostles.

The Spirit of God inspired you to write your Epistle on the Word that brings life and to witness to the truth of it by the shedding of your blood.

Obtain for me from the Giver of every good and perfect gift the graces I need.

Help me to treasure in my heart the good news of Jesus Christ and to strive by my life to bring others to its saving power. Amen.

Georges de la Tour. *St. Jude Thaddeus,* (1593-1652)
Musee Toulouse-Lautrec, Albi, France

The Way of the Cross

The Way of the Cross

The Way of the Cross is a devotion in which we meditate upon the passion of Christ. Through this devotion, we can experience Jesus' suffering as he made his way to Calvary, and feel his love – a love so great that he was willing to die for both ourselves and his Father. If we can begin to understand the human experience of suffering out love for one another, we will then begin to understand the meaning of the cross.

The Stations of the Cross
Opening Prayer

All-loving God, I raise my mind and heart to you in praise. Though weak and at times sinful I wish to follow your Son, Jesus, on the way of the cross.

May this meditation enable me to imitate in my own life the love with which he gave himself to you and to all his brothers and sisters. Amen.

Giovanni Bellini. *Christ Carrying the Cross*, (c.1505-10)
Isabella Stewart Gardner Museum, Boston, Massachusetts, USA

FIRST STATION
Jesus is condemned to death

The high priest rose before the assembly and questioned Jesus, saying, "Have you no answer? What are these men testifying against you?" But he was silent and answered nothing. Again the high priest asked him and said to him, "Are you the Messiah, the son of the Blessed One?" Then Jesus answered, "I am; and 'you will see the Son of Man seated at the right hand of the Power and coming with the clouds of heaven.' " At that the high priest tore his garments and said, "What further need have we of witnesses? You have heard the blasphemy. What do you think?" They all condemned him as deserving to die.

Mark 14:60-64

Lord Jesus Crucified, have mercy on me.

SECOND STATION
Jesus carries his Cross

When Pilate heard these words he brought Jesus out and seated him on the judge's bench in the place called Stone

Pavement, in Hebrew, Gabbatha. It was preparation day for Passover, and it was about noon. And he said to the Jews, "Behold, your king!" They cried out, "Take him away, take him away! Crucify him!" Pilate said to them, "Shall I crucify your king?" The chief priests answered, "We have no king but Caesar." Then he handed him over to them to be crucified. So they took Jesus, and carrying the cross himself he went out to what is called the Place of the Skull, in Hebrew, Golgotha.

John 19:13-17

Lord Jesus Crucified, have mercy on me.

THIRD STATION
Jesus falls the first time

Jesus said: "If the world hates you, realize that it hated me first. If you belonged to the world, the world would love its own; but because you do not belong to the world, and I have chosen you out of the world, the world hates you. Remember the word I spoke to you, 'No slave is greater than his master.' If they persecuted me, they will also persecute you. If they kept my word, they will also keep yours."

John 15:18-20

Lord Jesus Crucified, have mercy on me.

FOURTH STATION
Jesus meets his afflicted mother

Standing by the cross of Jesus were his mother and his mother's sister, Mary the wife of Clopas, and Mary of Magdala. When Jesus saw his mother and the disciple there whom he loved, he said to his mother, "Woman, behold, your son." Then he said to the disciple, "Behold, your mother." And from that hour the disciple took her into his home.

John 19:25-27

Lord Jesus Crucified, have mercy on me.

FIFTH STATION
Simon of Cyrene helps Jesus to carry his Cross

And when they had mocked him, they stripped him of the purple cloak, dressed him in his own clothes, and led him out to crucify him. They pressed into service a passer-by, Simon, a Cyrenian, who was coming in from the country, the father of Alexander and Rufus, to carry his cross. They brought him to the place of Golgotha (which is translated Place of the Skull).

Mark 15:20-22

Lord Jesus Crucified, have mercy on me.

SIXTH STATION
Veronica wipes the face of Jesus

"Then the king will say to those on his right, 'Come, you who are blessed by my Father. Inherit the kingdom prepared for you from the foundation of the world"...Then the righteous will answer him and say, 'Lord, when did we see you hungry and feed you, or thirsty and give you drink? When did we see you a stranger and welcome you, or naked and clothe you? When did we see you ill or in prison, and visit you?' And the king will say to them in reply, 'Amen, I say to you, whatever you did for one of these least brothers of mine, you did for me.'

Matthew 25:34, 37-40

Lord Jesus Crucified, have mercy on me.

SEVENTH STATION
Jesus falls the second time

Yet it was our infirmities that he bore, our sufferings that he endured, while we thought of him as stricken, as one smitten by God and afflicted. But he was pierced for our offenses, crushed for our sins. Upon him was the chastisement that makes us whole, by his stripes we were healed. We had all gone astray like sheep, each following his own way; But the LORD laid upon him the guilt of us all.

Isiah 53:4-6

Lord Jesus Crucified, have mercy on me.

EIGHTH STATION
Jesus meets the women of Jerusalem

A large crowd of people followed Jesus, including many women who mourned and lamented him. Jesus turned to them and said, "Daughters of Jerusalem, do not weep for me; weep instead for yourselves and for your children."

Luke 23:27-28

Lord Jesus Crucified, have mercy on me.

NINTH STATION
Jesus falls a third time

Jesus said, "... because I came down from heaven not to do my own will but the will of the one who sent me. And this is the will of the one who sent me, that I should not lose anything of what he gave me, but that I should raise it [on] the last day."

John 6:38-39

Lord Jesus Crucified, have mercy on me.

TENTH STATION
Jesus is stripped of his clothes

They gave Jesus wine to drink mixed with gall. But when he had tasted it, he refused to drink. After they had crucified him, they divided his garments by casting lots.

Matthew 27:34-35

Lord Jesus Crucified, have mercy on me.

ELEVENTH STATION
Jesus is nailed to the Cross

When they came to the place called the Skull, they crucified him and the criminals there, one on his right, the other on his left.

[Then Jesus said, "Father, forgive them, they know not what they do."] They divided his garments by casting lots. The people stood by and watched; the rulers, meanwhile, sneered at him and said, "He saved others, let him save himself if he is the chosen one, the Messiah of God." Even the soldiers jeered at him. As they approached to offer him wine they called out, "If you are King of the Jews, save yourself." Above him there was an inscription that read, "This is the King of the Jews."

Luke 23:33-38

Lord Jesus Crucified, have mercy on me.

TWELFTH STATION
Jesus dies on the cross

It was now about noon and darkness came over the whole land until three in the afternoon because of an eclipse of the sun. Then the veil of the temple was torn down the middle. Jesus cried out in a loud voice, "Father, into your hands I commend my spirit"; and when he had said this he breathed his last.

Luke 23:44-46

Lord Jesus Crucified, have mercy on me.

THIRTEENTH STATION
The body of Jesus is taken down from the Cross

But when they came to Jesus and saw that he was already dead, they did not break his legs, but one soldier thrust his lance into his side, and immediately blood and water flowed out. After this, Joseph of Arimathea, secretly a disciple of Jesus for fear of the Jews, asked Pilate if he could remove the body of Jesus. And Pilate permitted it. So he came and took his body.

John 19:33-34, 38

Lord Jesus Crucified, have mercy on me.

FOURTEENTH STATION
Jesus is laid in the tomb

Taking the body, Joseph wrapped it [in] clean linen and laid it in his new tomb that he had hewn in the rock. Then he rolled a huge stone across the entrance to the tomb and departed.

Matthew 27:59-60

Lord Jesus Crucified, have mercy on me.

Prayers to the Blessed Virgin Mary

The Regina Caeli
"Queen of Heaven"

Queen of heaven, rejoice, Alleluia.
The Son whom you were privileged
   to bear,
Alleluia, has risen as he said,
   Alleluia.
Pray to God for us, Alleluia.
Rejoice and be glad, Virgin Mary,
   Alleluia.
For the Lord has truly risen. Alleluia.
Let us pray.
O God it was by the Resurrection of
   your Son, our Lord Jesus Christ,
   that you brought joy to the world.
Grant that through the intercession of
   the Virgin Mary, his Mother, we may
   attain the joy of eternal life.
Through Christ, our Lord.
Amen.

The Memorare

Remember,
 O most gracious Virgin Mary,
 that never was it known that
 anyone who fled to your
  protection,
 implored your help,
 or sought your intercession
 was left unaided.
Inspired by this confidence,
 we fly unto you,
 O Virgin of virgins, our Mother!
To you we come,
 before you we stand,
 sinful and sorrowful.
O Mother of the Word incarnate,
 despise not our petitions,
 but in your mercy hear and
 answer us.
 Amen.

The Angelus

The angel of the Lord declared
 unto Mary.
And she conceived of the Holy Spirit.
 Hail Mary…
Behold the handmaid of the Lord.
Be it done to me according to your
 word. Hail Mary…
And the Word was made flesh;
 and dwelt among us. Hail Mary…
Pray for us, O holy Mother of God,
 that we may be made worthy
 of the promises of Christ.
Let us pray.
Pour forth, we beseech you, O Lord,
 your grace in our hearts, that we,
 to whom the Incarnation of Christ,
 your Son, was made known by
 the message of an angel, may by
 his passion and cross be brought
 to the glory of his resurrection;
 through the same
Christ our Lord.
Amen.

Bartolome Esteban Murillo. *The Annunciation*,
Prado, Madrid, Spain

Raphael (Raffaello Sanzio of Urbino). *The Visitation*,
Prado, Madrid, Spain

Prayer of St. Francis de Sales

O most holy Mary, Virgin Mother of God, even though I am most unworthy to be your servant, I am moved by your motherly care for me and long to serve you.
I choose you this day to be my Queen, my Advocate, and my Mother, and I firmly resolve to always be devoted to you and to do what I can to encourage others to be devoted to you.
My loving Mother, through the precious Blood of your Son that was shed for me, I beg you to receive me as your eternal servant.
Aid me in my actions and beg for me the grace never by word, deed, or thought to be displeasing in either your sight or that of your most holy Son.
Remember me, dearest Mother, and do not abandon me at the hour of my death.

Prayer of St. Louis de Montfort

Hail Mary, beloved Daughter of the eternal Father, wonderful Mother of the Son, faithful Spouse of the Holy Spirit.

You are my loving Lady, my powerful Queen.

You are all mine through your mercy, and I am all yours.

Take away everything from me that may be displeasing to God.

Cultivate in me everything that is pleasing to you.

May the light of your faith dispel the darkness of my mind, your deep humility replace my pride; your continual sight of God fill my memory with his presence; and the fire of your heart, inflame the lukewarmness of my own heart.

May your virtues take the place of my sins, and may your merits be my enrichment to make up for all that is wanting in me before God.

Sandro Botticelli. *The Virgin Teaching the Infant Jesus to Read*, Museo Poldi Pezzoli, Milan, Italy

My beloved Mother, grant that I may
have no other spirit than yours,
that I know Jesus Christ and his
divine will and that I glorify the
Lord. Hail Mary, my dear
Mother, may I love God with a
burning love like yours.

Prayer of St. Thomas Aquinas

O Virgin full of goodness,
the Mother of mercy,
I entrust my body and soul,
my thoughts, my actions,
and my life and death to you.
O my Queen, help me, and deliver
me from the grasp of the devil.
Obtain for me the grace of loving
my Lord Jesus Christ, your Son,
with a true and perfect love.
And after him, O Mary, obtain for
me that same grace, so that I may
love you with all my heart and
above all things.

The Magnificat

My soul proclaims the greatness of
 the Lord and my spirit exults in
 God my savior; because he has
 looked upon his lowly handmaid.
Yes, from this day forward all
 generations will call me blessed,
 for the Almighty has done great
 things for me.
Holy is his name, and his mercy reaches
 from age to age for those
 who fear him.
He has shown the power of his arm,
 he has routed the proud of heart.
He has pulled down princes from
 their thrones and exalted the lowly.
The hungry he has filled with good
 things, the rich sent empty away.
He has come to the help of Israel
 his servant, mindful of his mercy –
 according to the promise he made
 to our ancestors – of his mercy to
 Abraham and to his descendants
 for ever.

Mary, Mother of Jesus

Litany of the Blessed Virgin Mary

Lord, have mercy,
Christ, have mercy,
Lord, have mercy.
Christ, hear us.
Christ, graciously hear us.
God, the Father of heaven,
    have mercy on us.
God, the Son,
    Redeemer of the world,
    have mercy on us.
God, the Holy Spirit,
    have mercy on us.
Holy Trinity, one God, have mercy
    on us.
Holy Mary, *(after each invocation, respond with, "Pray for us.")*
    – Pray for us.
Holy Mother of God,
Holy Virgin of virgins,
Mother of Christ,
Mother, full of grace,
Mother most pure,
Mother most chaste,

Immaculate Mother,
Sinless Mother,
Lovable Mother,
Model of Mothers,
Mother of good counsel,
Mother of our Maker,
Mother of our Savior,
Wisest of virgins,
Holiest of virgins,
Virgin, powerful in the sight of God,
Virgin, merciful to us sinners,
Virgin, faithful to all God asks of you,
Mirror of holiness,
Seat of wisdom,
Cause of our joy,
Shrine of the Spirit,
Honor of your people,
Devoted handmaid of the Lord,
Mystical rose,
Tower of David,
Tower of ivory,
House of gold,
Ark of the covenant,
Gate of heaven,
Star of hope,

Health of the sick,
Refuge of sinners,
Comfort of the afflicted,
Help of Christians,
Queen of angels,
Queen of patriarchs,
Queen of prophets,
Queen of apostles,
Queen of martyrs,
Queen of confessors,
Queen of virgins,
Queen of all saints,
Queen conceived in holiness,
Queen raised up to glory,
Queen of the rosary,
Queen of peace,
Lamb of God, you take away the sins of the world,
– Spare us, O Lord.
Lamb of God, you take away the sins of the world,
– Graciously hear us, O Lord.
Lamb of God, you take away the sins of the world,
– Have mercy on us.

Pray for us, O holy Mother of God,
> – That we may be made worthy of the promises of Christ.

Let us pray.
Lord our God,
in this great sacrament we come into the presence of Jesus Christ, your Son, born of the Virgin Mary and crucified for our salvation. May we who declare our faith in this fountain of love and mercy drink from it the water of everlasting life. We ask this through Christ our Lord.

Bartolome Esteban Murillo. *The Madonna of the Rosary*, Dulwich Picture Gallery, London, UK

The Rosary of the Blessed Virgin Mary

"To recite the Rosary is nothing other than to contemplate the face of Christ with Mary."

Pope John Paul II

The Rosary is the most popular of all the Marian devotions. It was revealed to St. Dominic by the Blessed Mother and begun in the fifteenth century by Alen de Rupe, a Dominican preacher. The Rosary combines both vocal and meditative prayer, and is treasured by all who use it.

On October 16, 2002, Pope John Paul II published an apostolic letter titled "Rosarium Virginis Mariae." He called on Catholics to pray the Rosary and enter "the school of Mary," who knew Jesus Christ so well as his mother and his closest disciple. Though it is not mandatory, the pope suggested additions to the traditional fifteen mysteries of the Rosary. They are the Luminous Mysteries, or the Mysteries of Light, which include the mysteries of Christ's public ministry between his Baptism and his Passion. While leaving the use of these mysteries to the freedom of individuals and communities, Pope John Paul suggested that they may help to make the Rosary be a prayer centered in the life of Christ. The complete Rosary consists of twenty decades, but is further divided into four distinct parts, each containing five decades called the Joyful, the Luminous, the Sorrowful, and the Glorious Mysteries. The Mysteries of the Rosary symbolize important events from the lives of both our Lord and the Blessed Mother.

Each decade contains one mystery, an "Our Father," ten "Hail Marys," and a "Glory be to the Father." To say the Rosary, begin by making the sign of the cross and saying "The Apostles' Creed" on the crucifix, one "Our Father" on the first bead, three "Hail Marys" on the next three beads, and then a "Glory be to the Father." When this is finished, meditate upon the first mystery, say an "Our Father," ten "Hail Marys," and one "Glory be to the Father." The first decade is now completed, and to finish the Rosary proceed in the same manner until all five decades have been said.

The Five Joyful Mysteries

Mondays and Saturdays

1. The Annunciation

The Angel Gabriel tells Mary that she is to be the Mother of God.

2. The Visitation

The Blessed Virgin pays a visit to her cousin Elizabeth.

3. The Nativity

The Infant Jesus is born in a stable at Bethlehem.

4. The Presentation

The Blessed Virgin presents the Child Jesus to Simeon in the Temple.

5. The Finding in the Temple

Jesus is lost for three days, and the Blessed Mother finds him in the Temple.

The Five Luminous Mysteries
Thursdays

1. The Baptism of Jesus

Jesus is baptized in the Jordan River by John the Baptist.

2. The Wedding at Cana

Jesus attends a wedding at Cana in Galilee, where he turns water into wine.

3. The Proclamation of the Kingdom of God

Jesus goes through the towns and cities of his own country proclaiming God's Kingdom and helping the poor.

4. The Transfiguration

Jesus leads his friends up a high mountain, where they see him shining in glorious light.

5. The Institution of the Holy Eucharist

At supper with his friends before he dies, Jesus gives himself to them in bread and wine.

The Five Sorrowful Mysteries
Tuesdays and Fridays

1. **The Agony in the Garden**
Jesus prays in the Garden of Olives and drops of blood break through his skin.

2. **The Scourging at the Pillar**
Jesus is tied to a pillar and cruelly beaten with whips.

3. **The Crowning with Thorns**
A crown of thorns is placed upon Jesus' head.

4. **The Carrying of the Cross**
Jesus is made to carry his cross to Calvary.

5. **The Crucifixion**
Jesus is nailed to the cross, and dies for our sins.

The Five Glorious Mysteries
Wednesdays and Sundays

1. **The Resurrection**
Jesus rises from the dead, three days after his death.
2. **The Ascension**
Forty days after his death, Jesus ascends into heaven.
3. **The Descent of the Holy Spirit**
Ten days after the Ascension, the Holy Spirit comes to the apostles and the Blessed Mother in the form of fiery tongues.
4. **The Assumption**
The Blessed Virgin dies and is assumed into heaven.
5. **The Crowning of the Blessed Virgin**
The Blessed Virgin is crowned Queen of Heaven and Earth by Jesus, her Son.

Hail, Holy Queen

Hail, holy Queen, mother of mercy, our life, our sweetness, and our hope. To you we cry, poor banished children of Eve; to you we send up our sighs, mourning and weeping in this valley of tears.
Turn then, O most gracious advocate, your eyes of mercy toward us, and after this our exile, show unto us the blessed fruit of your womb, Jesus.
O clement, O loving, O sweet Virgin Mary.
V. Pray for us, O holy Mother of God
R. That we may be made worthy of the promises of Christ.
Let us pray.
O God, whose only begotten Son, by his life, death, and resurrection, has purchased for us the rewards of eternal life, grant, we beseech you, that meditating upon these Mysteries of the most Holy Rosary of the Blessed Virgin Mary, we may imitate what they contain and obtain what they promise.
Through the same Christ our Lord. Amen.

Guercino (Giovanni Francesco Barbieri). *St. Joseph,* (1591-1666)
Palazzo Pitti, Florence, Italy

Prayers to St. Joseph

Prayer to St. Joseph

Loving St. Joseph, may your holy life be an inspiration to me when I find it difficult to be faithful in the fulfillment of my duties.

You are now glorified with Jesus and Mary and are a powerful intercessor at the throne of God.

Blessed foster-father of Jesus, extend to me the same tender care with which you protected Jesus and Mary that I may walk securely in the path of salvation.

Obtain for me strong faith, ardent love, and zeal in doing good. With Jesus and Mary, help me at the hour of my death so that I may partake of the complete redemption of the children of God and eternally praise the Father, Son, and Holy Spirit. Amen.

Prayer to St. Joseph, the Worker

Glorious St. Joseph, model of all who are dedicated to labor, obtain for me the grace to work in the spirit of love and faithfully to place my responsibilities above my own desires.
Help me to work with joy and gratitude.
Let me consider it an honor to use and develop the gifts I have received from God.
Aid me to work with order, peace, moderation, and patience.
Help me to work above all for the glory of God and the coming of his kingdom.
May I remember that I am to give an account of the gifts and talents I have received.

Prayer to St. Joseph for Others

St. Joseph, be my patron and intercessor with God.
Through the merits of Jesus and Mary obtain for me pardon of all my sins.
Implore for me a great purity of heart, a lively faith, firm hope, and perfect charity.
Help me in all my needs of soul and body but most of all in the hour of my death.
Come to me then with Jesus and Mary and let me die in their love and with the help of your prayers.
Glorious St. Joseph, powerful protector of holy Church, I implore your heavenly aid for the whole Church on earth, especially for the Holy Father and all bishops, priests, and religious.
Guide and help all government officials, comfort the afflicted, console the dying, and convert sinners. Have pity on all who have died especially members of my own family and friends.

Allow them to join you and the saints in the praise and glory of God.
Amen.

Prayer to St. Joseph for Strength

St. Joseph,
we confidently invoke your patronage.
By that charity with which you were united to the Immaculate Virgin Mother of God, and by that fatherly love with which you embraced the child Jesus, we beg you and humbly pray that you will look graciously upon the inheritance which Jesus Christ purchased by his blood and assist us in our need by your power and strength.
Most watchful guardian of the holy family, protect the chosen people of Jesus Christ.
Keep far from us, most loving father, all blight of error and corruption.
Mercifully help us from heaven, most valiant defender, in this conflict with

the powers of darkness. And even as of old you rescued the Child Jesus from the peril of his life, so now defend God's holy Church from the snares of the enemy and from all adversity.

Keep us one and all under your continual protection, that supported by your example and your help, we may lead a holy life, die a happy death, and come at last to the possession of everlasting blessedness in heaven.

Amen.

Prayer to St. Joseph

O Holy Joseph, chaste spouse of the Mother of God, most glorious advocate of all who are in danger or in their last agony, and most faithful protector of all the servants of Mary, I, in the presence of Jesus and Mary, do from this moment choose you for my powerful patron and advocate, and I implore you to obtain for me through your powerful intercession the grace of a happy death.

Receive me, therefore, as your perpetual servant, and recommend me to the constant protection of Mary, your spouse, and to the everlasting mercies of Jesus, my Savior.

Assist me in all the actions of my life, which I now offer to the greater glory of Jesus and Mary.

Never, therefore, forsake me; and whatsoever grace you see most necessary and profitable for me, obtain it for me now and also at the hour of my death.

I know not when I shall die, but whatsoever hour it shall happen I invite you to be with me at my deathbed.

Through your gracious intercession may there be granted me in my last hour all the graces I need, through the merits of Jesus Christ, my Savior, who together with the Father and the

Holy Spirit, lives and reigns, world without end. Amen.

Prayer to St. Joseph

Especially recommended to be said with the Rosary during October

To you, O blessed Joseph, we have recourse in our affliction; and having implored the help of your most holy Spouse, we confidently invoke your patronage also.

By that charity which bound you to the Immaculate Virgin, Mother of God, and by the fatherly love with which you embraced the Child Jesus, look down, we beseech you, with gracious eye on the precious inheritance which Jesus Christ purchased in his blood, and help us in our necessities by your power and aid.

Protect, O most watchful guardian of the Holy Family, the elect children of Jesus Christ; ward off from us, O most loving father, all blight of error and corruption; aid us from on high, O most valiant defender, in our struggle with the powers of darkness; and, even as of old you rescued the Child Jesus from the peril of his life, so now defend God's holy Church from the snares of the enemy and from all adversity.

Shield also each one of us by your constant protection, so that, supported by your example and your aid, we may live a holy life, die a happy death, and attain everlasting happiness in heaven. Amen.

Litany of St. Joseph

Lord, have mercy.
  Christ, have mercy.
  Lord, have mercy.
  Christ, hear us.
  Christ, graciously hear us.
  God, the Father of heaven,
      have mercy on us.
  God, the Son, Redeemer of the world,
      have mercy on us.
  God the Holy Spirit, have mercy on us.
  Holy Trinity, one God, have mercy on us.
  Holy Mary,   – Pray for us.
  St. Joseph, (*After each invocation, respond with "Pray for us."*)
  Renowned descendant of David,
  Light of patriarchs,
  Husband of the Mother of God,
  Chaste guardian of the Virgin,
  Foster-father of the Son of God,
  Watchful defender of Christ,
  Head of the holy family,
  Joseph, most just,
  Joseph, most pure,

Joseph, most prudent,
Joseph, most valiant,
Joseph, most obedient,
Joseph, most faithful,
Mirror of patience,
Lover of poverty,
Model of artisans,
Glory of domestic life,
Guardian of virgins,
Mainstay of families,
Consolation of those in trouble,
Hope of the sick,
Patron of the dying,
Protector of holy Church.
Lamb of God, you take away the sins of the world, – Spare us, O Lord.
Lamb of God, you take away the sins of the world,
– Graciously hear us, O Lord.
Lamb of God, you take away the sins of the world, – Have mercy on us.
He made him lord of his household,
– And ruler over all his possessions.
Let us pray.
God, in your infinite wisdom and love

you chose Joseph to be the husband of Mary, the Mother of your Son.
May we have the help of his prayers in heaven and enjoy his protection on earth.
We ask this through our Lord Jesus Christ, your Son, who lives and reigns with you and the Holy Spirit, one God, for ever and ever. Amen.

Litany of Humility

O Jesus meek and humble of heart, hear me.
From the desire of being esteemed,
(After each invocation, respond with, "Deliver me Jesus.")
From the desire of being loved,
From the desire of being extolled,
From the desire of being honored,
From the desire of being praised,
From the desire of being preferred to others,
From the desire of being consulted,
From the desire of being approved,
From the fear of being humiliated,

From the fear of being despised,
From the fear of suffering rebukes,
From the fear of being maligned,
From the fear of being forgotten,
From the fear of being ridiculed,
From the fear of being wronged,
From the fear of being suspected,
That others may be loved more than I,
(After each invocation, respond with, "Jesus, grant me the grace to desire it.")
That others may be esteemed more than I,
That in the opinion of the world, others may increase, and I may decrease,
That others may be chosen and I set aside,
That others may be praised and I unnoticed,
That others may be preferred to me in everything,
That others become holier than I, provided that I may become as holy as I should.

Cardinal Raphael Merry del Val